THAT POEM

written and illustrated by E. Alen

Illustrations were made using pen, pencil, watercolor, pastel, and acrylic paint, then touched up digitally.

Illustrations copyright © 2024 by E. Alen
Front cover image by E. Alen

ISBN: 979-8-9902169-2-1
Published in the United States of America
First published edition 2024.

Dana is the recipient of a very grand, gargantuan thank you from E. Alen.

THAT POEM

by E. Alen

TABLE OF CONTENTS

Chapter 1:
Where I Dream 1

The poems in this book have been compiled
over the course of twelve years.
These are some of my more memorable works
from that time.
I hope you enjoy.

~ E. Alen

Dedicated to the Reader

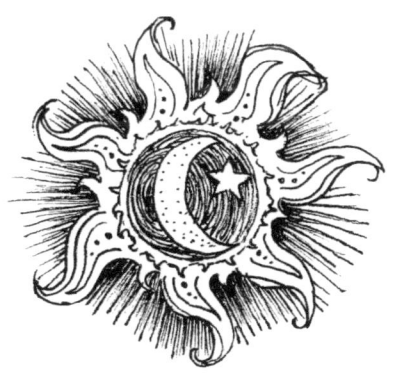

Chapter 1:

Where I Dream

Inside My Head

A million times I've stood there at the shore,
Yet I've never touched the sea,
And sometimes I just think:
What if I never stopped to breathe?
What if I just plunged into the water,
Even though that would've been harder,
But I would've learned how to swim on my own?
What if I didn't sit at the water's edge?
What if I didn't always sit inside my head?
Where would I swim? Where would I be?
If I could be free, if I could be free.

3

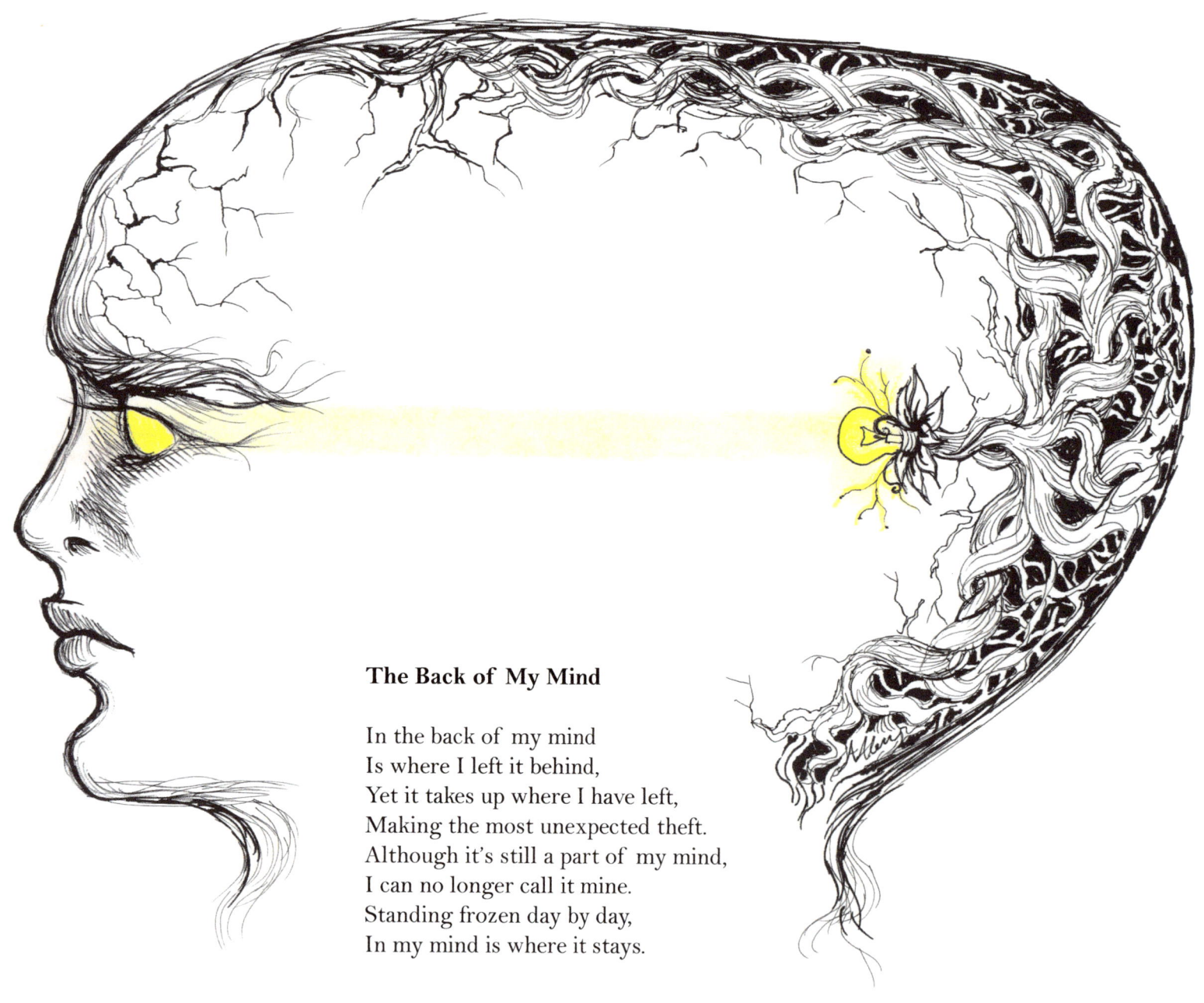

The Back of My Mind

In the back of my mind
Is where I left it behind,
Yet it takes up where I have left,
Making the most unexpected theft.
Although it's still a part of my mind,
I can no longer call it mine.
Standing frozen day by day,
In my mind is where it stays.

All in Good Time

Living is the absence of time,
Death is the silence of today.
Don't shake the leaves off your tree
Because they'll fall off anyway.

The Sun Still Comes

Maybe if I stay up just a little bit more,
Tomorrow won't come just yet,
But, of course, the sun still comes,
A fact I tend to forget.

6

New Page

I sharpen my pencil,
Study my thoughts
And try to untangle
All of its knots,

But I come up dry
Just like the paint.
Instead of pictures,
I'm drawing blanks.

But I don't care!
So I lay down the law,
I let go of my fears
And I let my hand draw,

I connect all the dots,
I unravel the riddle —
Yet when I was done —
All I saw was a scribble.

I had worked so hard
And it turned out a mess.
Why do I even try?
That's anyone's guess.

So I crumpled my paper
And scowled at my pen,
Looked at my new page,
And I started again.

The Silver Tree

In constant reach,
In constant reach,
The silver tree
You'll never teach.
Its limbs and trunk
Are made with steel
Each branch a blade
That severs yet feels.
Polished metal
Heeds no advice,
Fine and sharpened
It pays the price.
Clanging and tangling
Against one another
Branch against branch
Metal breaking each other
In constant reach,
In constant reach,
Those futile words
You'll always preach.

Loser

Your heart gets broken,
My heart's never touched.
You find love too little,
I find it too much.
You look to the sky,
I look left and right.
You stumble and fall,
And I keep upright.
You only shop windows,
And I only in stores,
I get coins from a pocket,
You get coins from the floor.
You have a blank for a path,
But a plan is my future
Because you are a dreamer,
And I'm just a loser.

Here

I feel guilty for standing here
For the thing that I got at dawn,
And now that it's already breathing here,
I can't let it be gone.
I know it's not my fault it's here
Because it was given to me.
The world would do so much better without it,
But I'm too selfish to set it free.

Drowners

You hold your breath underwater,
Accepting those long, aching hours,
Waiting to help and save those who sink,
Helping those unfortunate drowners,
Not knowing if any of it will ever come back,
But what stands as an equal to the honor?
That which seldom may be grasped
As it dissolves like sweat in the water.

12

Always Remembered

What I have mistaken for summer
Was always a stagnant day in winter,
Frozen and picturesque,
A snapshot to be put away
But always remembered
On every steadily sweltering summer day
As all things dry, crack,
And bright colors fade to gray.
My vision grows black,
My hands colder and stiffer,
Only to someday find it's spring again
Then look behind me and realize it was always winter.

Cold

The sun and clouds on the water
Broken leaves in a huddle
I look down and see
My reflection in a puddle.

A winter jacket zipped to my chin
A cold stone in my warm hand
An earthworm wriggling
And inching up the moist land.

The bare trees above me
The grass wet with dew
The sky crowded and cloudy
With a light grayish hue.

My nose cold and pink
The ground damp and cool
I take my stone and throw it
Into the shimmering clear pool.

My Big Sweater

I give up, I want my big sweater back,
Back when it was okay to just call it that,
But the sweater's already unraveling at the wrists,
Maybe I should just call it quits.
Because the sweater won't fit no matter how hard I try,
There's nowhere to turn, no place to hide.

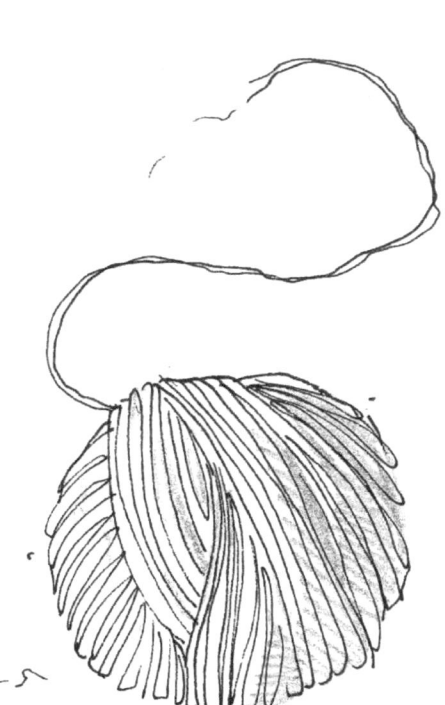

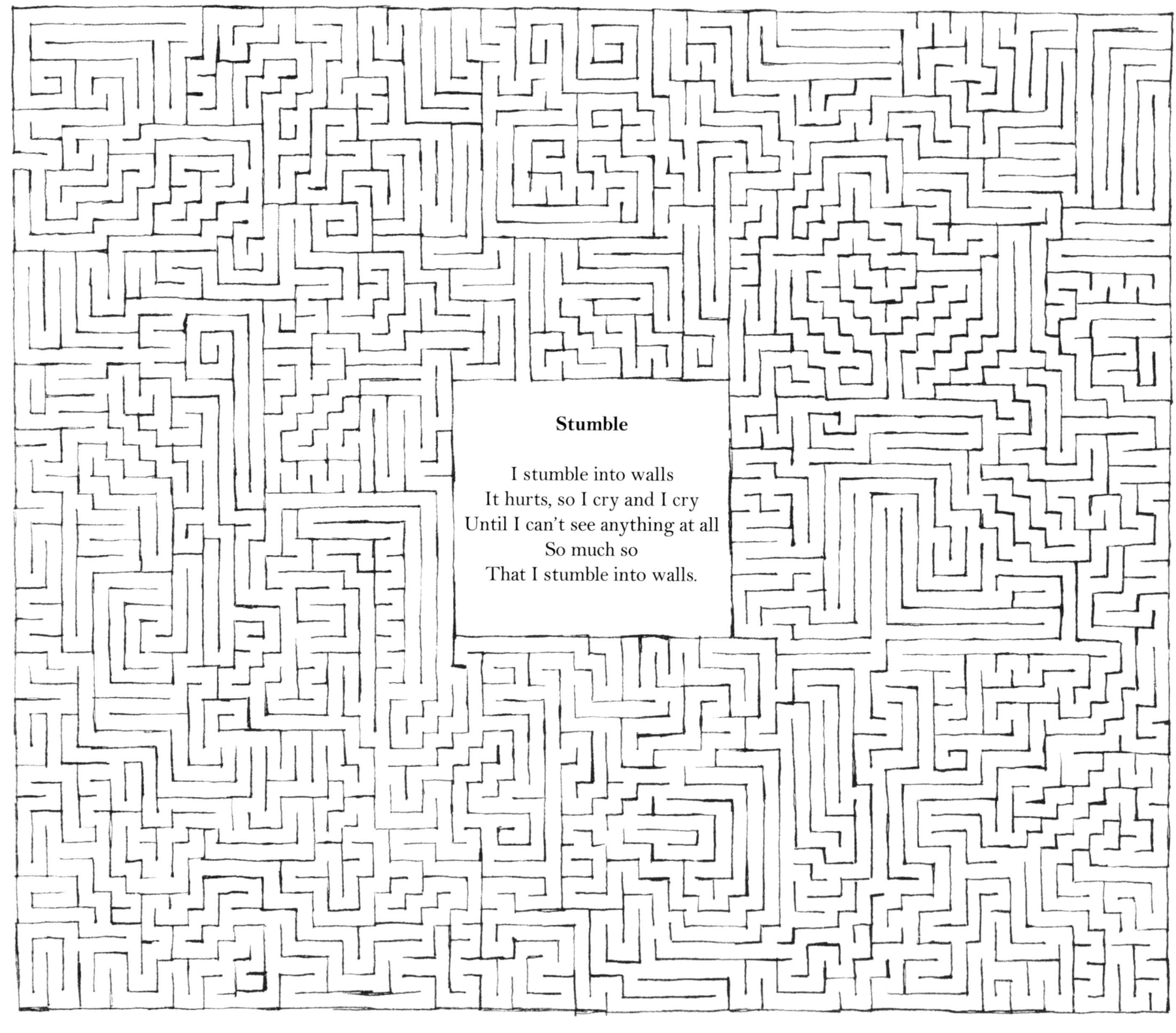

Stumble

I stumble into walls
It hurts, so I cry and I cry
Until I can't see anything at all
So much so
That I stumble into walls.

Listen to Them

Listen to them
They think I'm not here
So into the crack I peer.
Listen to them
They've been talking for years.

Little Polkadot

You're just like everyone else
And that's what's wrong with you.
Your problems are nothing original—
Come up with something new.
But I have nothing.
I have nothing except time—
No, might as well be everything,
Too much of everything on my mind.

LOST IN A CIRCLE

Around and around, and around and around I go and I go. This path is immutable, standing lost in a circle. Today, once more, all I am is another entry in a journal, standing lost in a circle. Around and around I go, and again I know, I might as well stop because if I go on I'll end up exactly where I started from.

Still, the pages turn, like a wheel—That was the deal: You can't return no matter how hard you dig in your heels. Still—something moves me, is it time? Or a state of mind? Somehow I move on to another entry in the journal, around and around and around, around in a circle. Around and around I go. Around and around and around.

What I Think

So, what do I think?
Well, I think they think I'm a failure,
And the failed—they think I'm a savior.
The givers think I'm ungrateful,
And to whom I give think I'm forgetful.
The sellers think I'm money,
And the rich think I am nothing.
The young think I'm just a baby,
And the old think I'm lazy.
The sighted think I'm hidden,
And the blind think I can't listen.
The collected think I quiver,
And who collects think I am quicker.
The heroes think I'm in need of help,
And the bitter think I should fend for myself.
The smart think I'm a sullen nitpicker,
And the dumb think I'm a thinker.
The people think they know me,
But even where it's clean,
The water's still soapy.
I thought I knew the people,
But they, too, disappoint me.
But, what do I think?
And that's exactly
What I think.

In-Betweeners

If it's not simple enough to be enjoyed
Or not enormous enough to be grieved,
Then it slips in, through the cracks,
And falls into the Between.
That horrible Between shows no mercy,
Nothing to guide you as you stumble underground
Because the ones who surround you
Are the in-betweeners too.
The in-betweeners are never found.
Lost to a kingdom beneath the light and dirt,
Entire generations who've forgotten their worth
Never to see the light of day, but,
Unless someone took a shovel to the earth,
It will be resigned to its grave
And in that between
It will stay.

If You Are Here

If you're here, with me,
Then maybe I'm not just talking to myself.
You might tell me something I don't know,
Maybe something I need to hear,
Before that wide expance before us,
In that distant place that's all too near,
In that instant where one of us might disappear.
Maybe there's a reason why I'm here—
If you are here, with me.

No Matter Where I Go

No matter where I go,
I will never be alone.
I'll be right there,
By my side.
No one knows me like I do,
Only I know what to do.
No matter where I go,
I will never be alone.

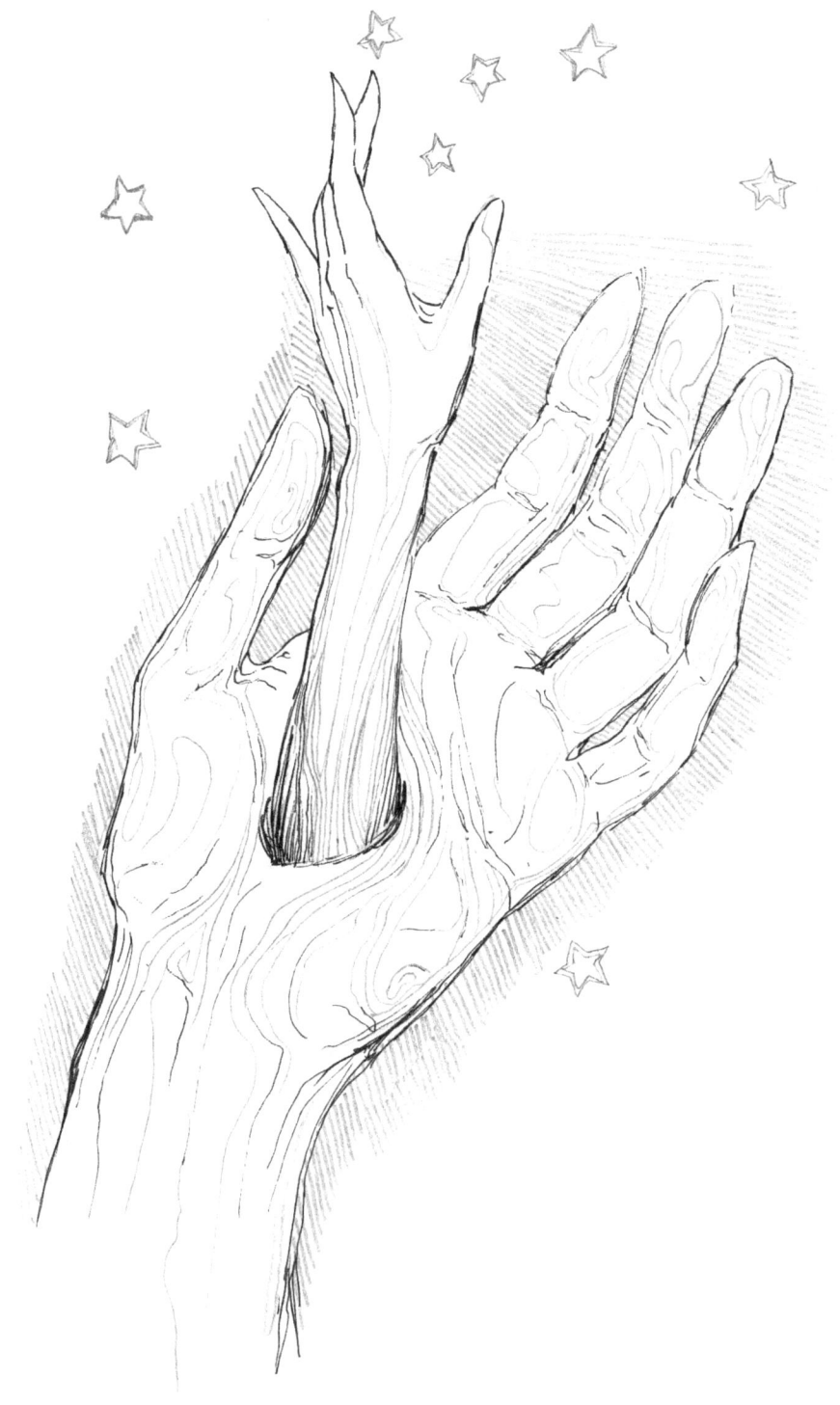

Just a Lonely Dream Seeking Shelter

"Hello,"
my sign says,
"I'm just a lonely dream seeking shelter."

The paper has become almost too soggy to hold,
And my nose and toes feel frozen out in the street,

My stomach complains of hunger,
And my shoulders sag with weariness and defeat.

My hat is now faded
And it's sagging under the weight of the water.
Some might say I'm very beautiful, if a little jaded,
If only I would stand a little taller.

I stand alone out in the rain,
Outside shops and banks and parks.
Some occasionally like to feed me,
Leaving bits or crumbs or chunks,
But no one actually wants to keep me,
Saying I'd expect a little too much.

And I guess they're right in that regard
Because I do enjoy putting you to the test.
I hate to be forgotten, you see,
Can they be more resilient than all the rest?

But I always find myself in the exact, same place:
Kicked out, back out in the street.
I stuff my hands inside my little pockets,
Kicking a little pebble with my cold feet.

I'll probably then pass some big, green park
And the dogs will lick my fingers,
Nudge at my clothes
As children will gather all around me,
Asking their parents,
Oh, could they *please*
Take this Lonely Dream home?

And parents will nod and say,
Of course,
But sometimes I can tell
That their smiles are a little forced.

But fine,
I will then go
From welcome stranger,
To best friend,
To somewhere in-between,
Until finally, I'll end up as an occasional visitor —
And even then,
Only up until they're eighteen.
Or maybe twenty, or thirty, or for—
—But the point is,

In the end, it's too much work
To keep a Dream.

So you'll find me in alleyways, in parks,
In front of shops or office dwellers,
"Hello," my sign will say,
"I'm just a lonely dream seeking shelter."

Chapter 2:

A Thousand Days Ago

Promise

Promise sounds familiar.
I think I said that yesterday.
But as time goes, time shows
That now is now today.
"Promise" isn't promised,
At least, with me that's how it is.
Unattainable goals and dreams
Then losing hope in a wish.
Promise always ends the same way —
It makes sense they never follow.
How can I promise myself today
If I am someone else tomorrow?

Dear Narrator

I'd wish to be my hero,
I'd wish for attention or wealth,
But who'd be interested in my story?
I'm only here to narrate to myself.
I'd wish for hearts or promises,
But they break time after time.
Who cares about my dreams?
Real life suits me just fine.

Fall Breathes

Fall breathes those wind-borne
So palms flee in blind swarms.
Only fingers are left behind
Looking for warmth they'll rarely find,
And if they did, they would grieve and weep
For without palms, what could you keep?
Even with a lonesome pull in us all,
The fear to feel finds us in the fall.

Fall breathes those wind-borne
And a shawl feels like home, worn,
Only it's too close to help unwind,
Our fingers clawing at its bind,
Overheating, buried under layers so deep,
But out in the cold, where would you sleep?
For even with a solar spirit in us all,
The fear to feel finds us in the fall.

Night Owl

I am a night owl
Living the life of an early bird.
Stretched out my claws,
But then pecked for the worm.

Lifeless living,
Living a life until some day when I die.
A dark, ocean blue
Living a lie behind the sunlit sky.

Morning Comes Too Soon

Morning comes too soon
As I stare out the window.
Maybe it's sundown's rotten humor
Or a daytime's early bloomer,
But the thief that left me blind
Is the one I cannot find,
Never mind the sunlit past
Because the morning comes too fast.
Spend the night searching long
Only to find that you were wrong.
That the answers cannot come free
If at night you cannot see.
As I stare out the window,
Morning comes too soon.

In The Bottle

I wish
I could be peaceful,
To be steady and still
Like a great rock in
The ocean. To enjoy
The lap of the waves
But not be swept up
In its emotion.
And

I wish to be strong,
Wish I were sure
And unruly
Like a wild wind
On the beach.
To be impossible to
Bottle or calm,
Yet to have the entire
World in my palm,
With everything
within reach.

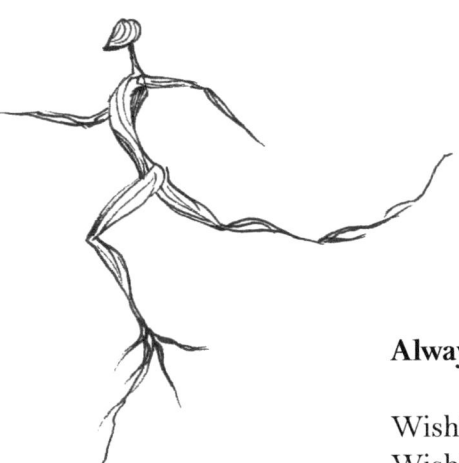

Always Dream

Wishing for the unknown,
Wishing for the unseen,
But however far you run,
The horizon stays at bay—
Ah, but one can always dream.

Your dreamy eyes will see
Only what you see.
Too bad, it's impossible
To wish for what you have—
But one can always dream.

And though I share in your wonder,
Not all things are what they seem.
I wish you could be happier
With where you are now—
But one will always dream.

A Candlelight Flickering

With a forever faltering confidence,
A candlelight flickering, dying, coming, then going,
Trying so pathetically,
Looking longingly to the leonine fire in the hearth,
Convinced it cannot fulfill the wish that sits inside its heart.
No more than a lone, blinking, watery flame,
Knowing that if it pinches itself out
The lighting in the room would still stay the same.
Surrounded by fire and fear,
Perfection calls and pulls at its chains.
But it's all such a lie, and even
If it were true,
Nothing would ever change.

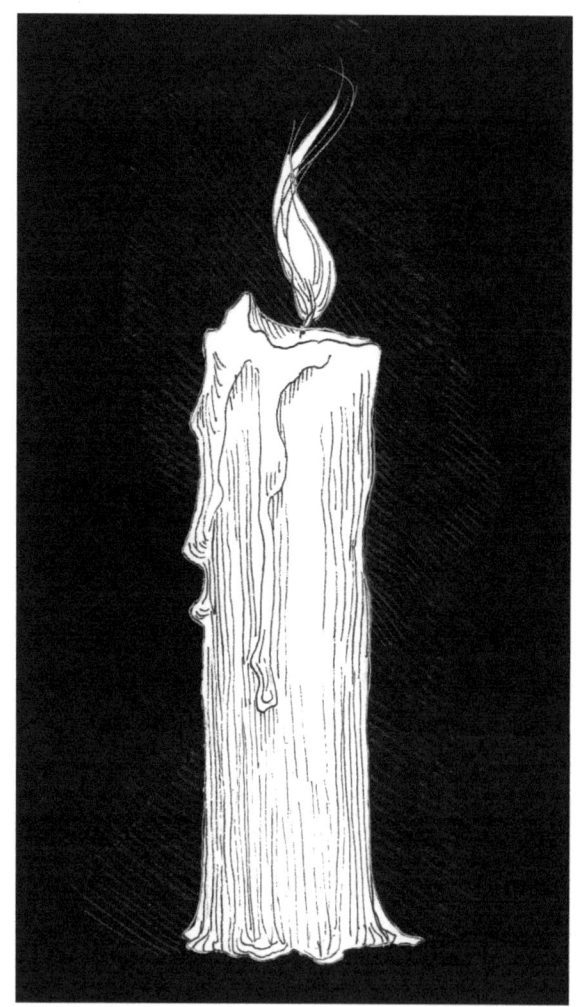

Always New Moon

I am your moon
And you are my sun,
Without you, I am no one.
And, when you'll explode and disappear,
I'll be left wanting and poor,
Lamenting in cold misery
How no one knows me anymore.
Your light has left me too fascinated
To know I've been overshadowed
Through the illusion of being illuminated.
I wish I'd have went on further, farther,
But my reflection is what I've always debated;
Maybe not whether or not it was there,
But how I could've changed it.

Sweeter Smile

I swallow down my bitterness like a pill.
The taste of it burns like bile
Making way for that
Sought after sweeter smile.

My potion like another's poison
That others have withstood,
A taste of my own medicine
Would serve me some good.

So I take this pill, I take this pill,
That promises to take care
Of the emptiness I could never fill.

So I swallow down my bitter pill
And the taste of it burns like bile
Making way for that
Sought after sweeter smile.

King

End the evil.
Without or with names, fate tomorrow reveals intention,
Then down you take dissensions! King,
You name its changed game, the trace
You looked over—
Fortune so bold, the shackled defeated,
While sin couldn't crumble you.
You judge others. You know who those, there,
Are all around— Screeching beast—
This you see and breathe.
But I kid.
A just king, aren't you?
But,
But,
You aren't King.
Just a kid.
I but breathe and see you, this beast,
Screeching around all!
Are there those who know you?
Others judge you, you crumble.
Couldn't sin while defeated?—
Shackled the bold, so fortune overlooked you.
Trace the game, changed its name, you King!
Dissensions take you down, then intention reveals:
Tomorrow, fate names,
With or without evil:
The end.

Naught Ink a Butter

I kner naught ink a butter what I sayer,
Nor what comes from the naysayer
In my head, so like a fool, cowed,
I write to hear in here instead,
'Till words spill un-fearing, unbidden
And bleed like a pen. Dough may
Anon this mays the sent, still I
Regret
Everything I've said.

Between the careless lines, it reads:
Do not dare mistake these words for art,
Do not dare describe them as anything but,
And although the words don't make much sense,
This sort of nonsense tends to spurt from the heart.

But having have said all that,
Ignore these sore, pitiful words.
I kner naught ink a butter
What I sayer.
Never no not interesting, though,
How sounding soul incoherent
May once seem sew mourn brilliant?
So much mure ssrrrrrmarter,
However oft naught ink a butter.

The Boy

The little man sat down on the grass
And took off his old shoes;
"I wish I'd chosen differently
Had I'd known just what to choose."
The little man threw them far beyond us
And sat down once again.
"And yet, I would've never worn them
Had I'd known what's up ahead."

Life is a Party

Life is a party.
I'll hear the music at home,
Within walls or beyond,
Wherever I'll go.

At best attention seeking,
And at worst drunk and reeking,
Life is a party with whomever you're speaking.

Within each smile there's teeth,
With each cake comes a knife,
There's never a dull moment
In the party of life.

A Poet at the Party

Who needs a loner for a friend?
Who needs a thinker for a lover?
Who needs the poet at the party?
Who needs the ugly when you suffer?
Who needs games once you've grown?
Who needs stories when there's truth?
Who needs dreams when no one knows?
Who sees the moon when it's new?
I wonder, who needs the poet?
Who needs the poet,
A faceless moon,
The loner, the ugly?
And yet...
And yet without it all,
I'd be nowhere,
Not even at the party.

Without Our Skin

Holding hands is never the same without our skin,
Although we say we like to see what's within.
But it won't be the same as what we know,
Because we change no matter what we've shown —
Yet nothing can tell me that I won't be free
If I'm the one who lives within me,
So if I'm changed without the skin in which I live,
Promise me you'll accept the hand that I give.

Bare Hands

Your bones are only as strong
As the teeth that you bare,
And you're only as tough
As the skin that you wear,
And you're only as tall
As the hand that will reach,
And you're only as challenged
As the words that you preach.

Lost at Sea

The sun can't burn me,
My heart is made of steel.
Even lost at sea,
My chest filled with tears—
My heart could never feel.

But the sun will fade
And clouds will settle over it like dust,
My heart having stopped its weeping
And turned into rust.

Great Clouds

Fascinating, far, and forever shifting creatures:
Great clouds lost to the wind,
Great clouds forever painting pictures,
Never caring whether their art could be captured
Because even if you could touch them,
They'd evade and envelope you like vapor.
And you'd look up,
You'd be misty-eyed
For those heavy, great clouds imprisoned in the sky.
Is it really freedom? —
Drifting along the breeze? —
All while they soar far and farther
Than the horizon or I would ever see.

51

A Thousand Days Ago

A thousand days ago
I've been in here and I wrote different words,
Not words I'd use now,
Only the few I had known.
The story sounds different with that limited vocabulary,
Yet the context has stayed the same,
Or maybe my memory is the distorted one
Since now I'd call the same story by a different name?
A thousand days ago I was in a completely different place.

A hundred days ago, I might've told you who I am,
But a thousand days ago—
The memory has slipped away like sand.
Knowledge, I see now, never grows,
It only morphs and takes on a different form
Because the things that held my interest—
I can't understand them like I had before.
I am not smarter,
Only smarter in a different way,
While knowledge from a thousand days before
Has long slipped away.

Give me an opportunity some thousand days ago
And I'd have stuck to where I excelled,
Yet give the same opportunity to me now
And I would try something else.
A thousand days ago
I've been in here and said things
That I thought would forever be a part of me,
But now I know I can't remember reality,
Only that distant thing I call a memory
From a thousand days ago.

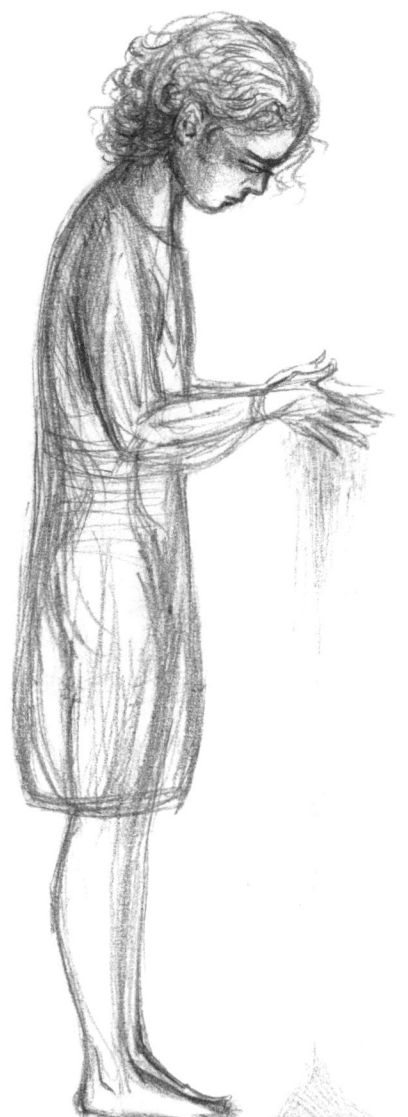

Chapter 3:

The Lonely Place

Smells of Home

This soup is empty.
This soup is warm, but empty.
Not quite filling, but heavy,
It sinks low into your belly.
And the soup has no beets,
No beans, no tomato.
No cabbage, no potato.
It has no carrots, no celery,
No herbs, no words,
No labor, no love,
No special, homey touch.
This soup is empty,
And it sits all alone,
And it never grows cold.
It is a soup full of nothing,
So it never grows old.
And it is so full of nothing,
You must take care
Not to spill any
Into the air.
But it smells of home,
And it's warm.
But it's empty, sitting heavy
Down deep inside your belly.

The Lonely Place

It is
Vacant
And overloooked.
I'm there
Where

Not another soul
Has set foot.
It is a strange land,
As I often

Walk in some
Lonely place
That not many
Will understand.

Though, there were times
When I wished that you
Could've helped me
Feel less alone,

But I guess you were
In a lonely place
Of your own.

Now I know
You need not go
To great lengths
To feel alone.

Life, sometimes,
Is a lonely place
Each only knows
As their own.

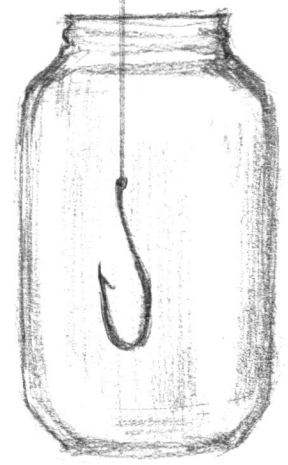

Perfect

A tall, looming
Shadow
That splays its shinning claws;
The painful awareness
Of all of my flaws.

A smile
That remembers
A thousand old tears;
The mighty strength
Made stronger by my fears.

A clean
That is never clean,
A nightmare that haunts me
Towards a dream,

To meet, at last,
Some kind of ideal,
To finally
Become something
That I will never feel.

Silly Goose

I was the silly goose
Who fell in love with the swan.
I couldn't have aimed any farther
Without leaving this desolate pond...

Your image had drifted to me upon the ripples
Amid fallen leaves and glaring sunlight.
Your broken reflection
Crowned me as your artist
And called me to write.

Like discovering there was a warmth
In the evening breeze,
Or a glowing, quiet moon in the night—
Whether you were looking or not,
I found myself in your eyes.

But like the way with all swans,
You were the star of a world
In which I never belonged.

And when I'd look down into the pond,
I could never see myself with you.
Have I never had a reflection?
Or did even the water think...

That I was too blue?
Like discovering there was a filth to your world,
Smelling of mildew and leaves—
The same world in which you reside.
What do I hate more? What do I love?
If I could, I'd search for the truth

In its lies.
But how could I say, what could I say?
How could I regret what's never been?
Whatever this is...

—What is this?
Is this...
    Love?
Euphoria...
    ...Confusion?
Poetry?
Or...

...An illusion?
Wondering whether destiny is it's own entity,
Whether tomorrow exists without today,
Or whether this pond was made from tears,
Whether all green had sprung from decay...
But, no matter what they tell you — it's love,

Not fate.
They'll tell you to throw caution to the wind,
Then leave you to pick up the pieces,
But I am safer here, in my own world.
It is they who do not listen.
No,

I was the goose who fell in love with the swan.
It was silly, I was foolish...
I was in the wrong.

I was the silly goose
Who fell in love with the swan.
I couldn't have aimed any farther
Without leaving this desolate pond.

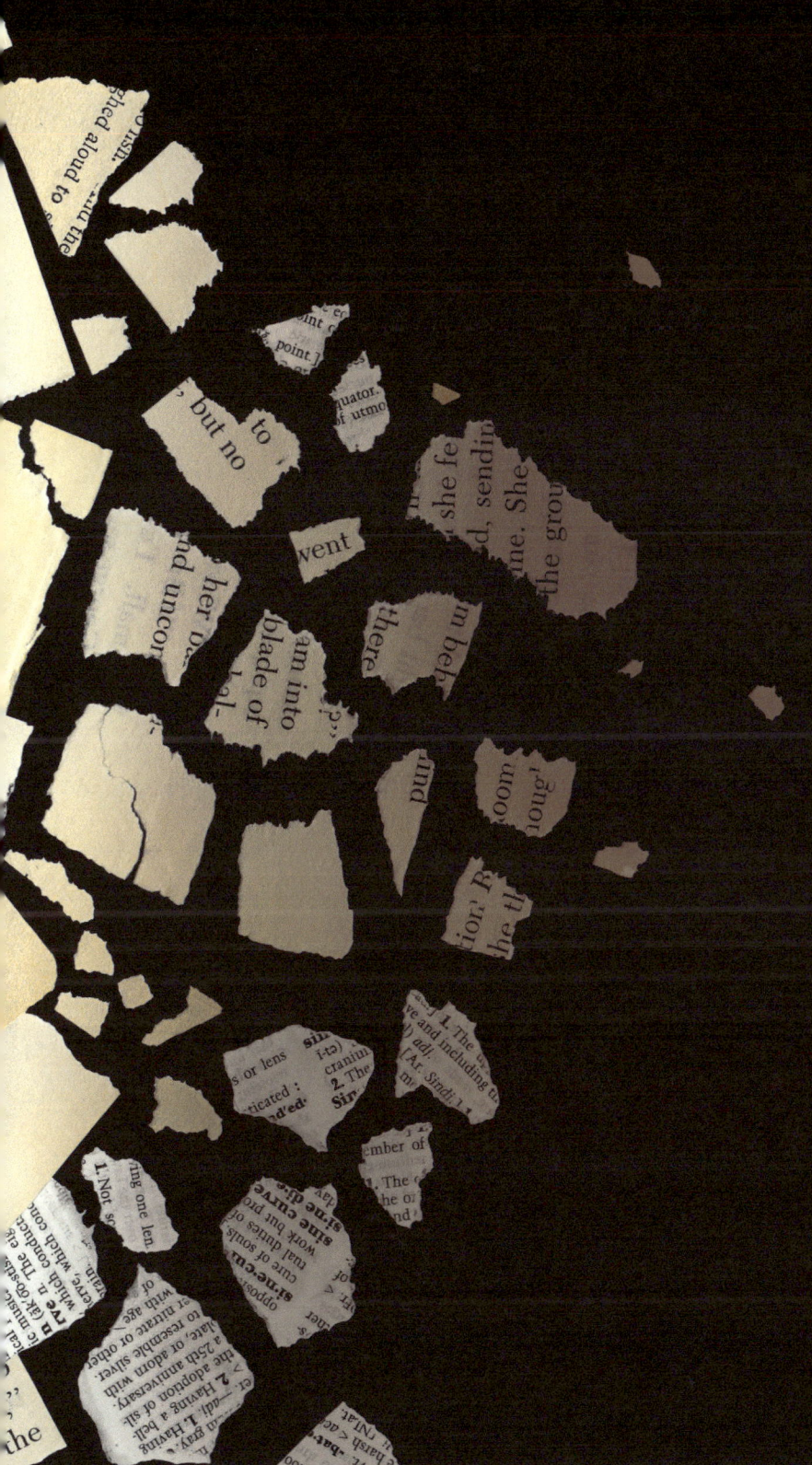

Bookworm

How slowly I seem to age.
Grow in bulk with each accumulative
Page. Snaking sentences,
I writhe and weave through a story long
And compact, crammed and compressed
Like an intestinal tract. What a tiresome
Journey to the end.
It will at last close shut,
Pressed flat and flush—
And never be seen again.

How small it will seem, but how wide,
Boundless and open it began.
From at the first to the last, why is the path
So long? Cover to cover—the distance
Is truly small. Seems along the way,
I meander, bend and wend.
Such an inefficient way to get to the end.

How sudden it will seem. How unfathomable,
But really, what a bore. The past will catch up to me,
The pages will grow closer, and the distance between them
Will grow shorter and shorter.

But my time until then
Stretches into forever
As I slither, so sinuous, so slow,
Worming through the serpentine rows,
Writing as if the words write themselves,
Wondering just what may lie beyond the bend...
How I wriggle and crawl
Bit by bit towards the edge...
Before turning... in a daze...
To move on sluggishly to the next.

Tongue

I am eaten up by fear.
Maybe, in many ways, I am not here.
Left only bones, remnants and crumbs.
It has eaten my flesh, my tongue.
I've been plunged into darkness,
Piecing together what's left to know—
But really, there's nowhere I can go.
I am only what fear has allowed of me,
What it's made of me.

I am eaten up by fear.
I am not here, I'm a ghost—
I am engulfed— Swallowed by fear,
I live my life looking out of its throat.

I fear,
I fear, I disappear
Deeper into my shell, eaten by it, by me,
Until all that's left is the shell
Of who I used to be.

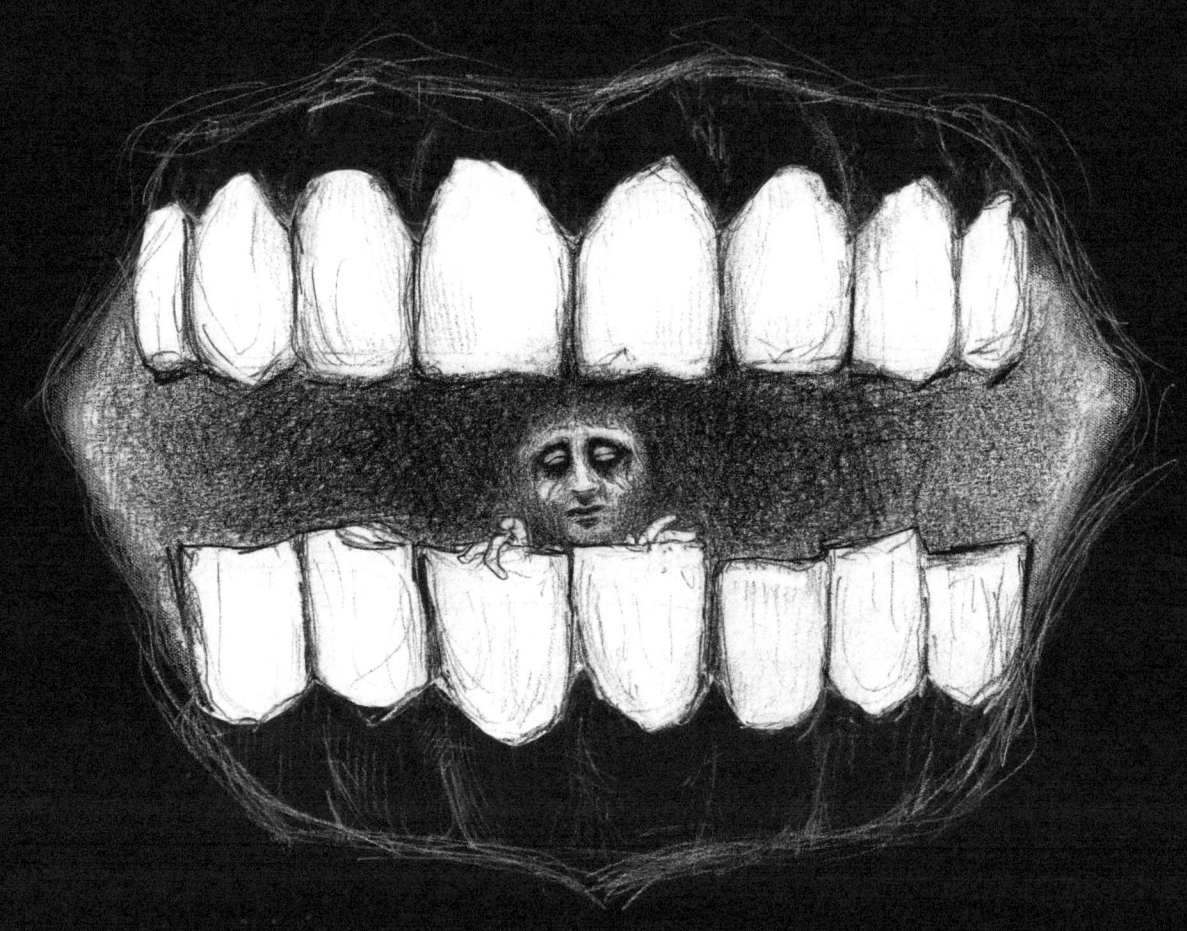

Window into my Soul

Do you think
That I am broken?
That I fool nobody, that I am broken,
Can you tell that I am broken?
Tell me,
Do you see the dirt
From the past
Seeping through the cracks?
Can you tell that I am broken?
Falling apart, cracking open —
Do you see the depth of my emotion?
Tell me,
Do you see a window
Into my soul?
Or do you just see a gaping,
Jagged hole?
Do you see me as broken?
Do you see the life I haven't lived?
Feel all the words I wish I'd said?
Do you find me unfeeling? Cold or numb —
Can you tell I'm desperately grasping
For the attention I'm fleeing from?
Tell me,
Do you understand
The words that cannot be spoken?
Can you tell that I am broken?

The Messenger

All the world is fraught
Inside the pocket
Where one single answer
Swims among a myriad of
Anxieties and disasters.

The seeker is bold
Grasping for a feeble hold
On times lost or bygone
Where the search for another's hand
Finds none who'd understand
Inside the pocket
Where all the world
Is quiet and withdrawn.

Chase

Some people
Call you talented
But what some might call talent
Is sometimes a matter of taste;

If I was after chasing perfection,
I wouldn't even know what to chase—
Because what some might call mistakes
Are sometimes the miserably hopeful
Scrawls and scribblings of a poor writer
Who didn't know what to erase.

Which path should I take?
It all keeps me awake.
But I unburden myself to none,
Wondering what I should've done.

Because it's hard to know when you're wrong
And even harder to know when you're right.

And the good and bad, they overlap.
The gray between is murky and vast—
Because the world isn't so black and white,
And you can't avoid the shadows
By simply stepping into the light.

The scrawls and scribblings of a poor writer
Who didn't know if it was all a mistake.
What an unlucky lucky treasure,
Some might call a waste,
Chasing after perfection,
Not knowing what to chase.

Checking Out

my life is a movie
and I sit watching it
in the theater alone. I
feel like I've seen this movie
before. they don't make them
how they used to do them anymore.
and all of these stories are all the same,
and they keep making the same mistakes,
and this picture remains unmoving, whether
it's colored or it's gray —when really? all I want
is something crazy, something really insane. I want
a movie that takes me out of my brain, I need something
out of this world, out of place —
I need this something to meet my gaze
and know me as surely as I know its face.
yet, out of all those people up there on the
screen, who's the one down here with me?
who's beside me in the darkness?
I look, and I meet no one's stare.
no, I only have a whole room
to myself with nobody to
care, and if they did,
would they still care?
and if I'm watching,
then am I nothing?
and if that's the
movie, then
what's this?
you know
what?
forget the
movie. I don't
care if it's not even
over yet. I think I'll just
leave. I think, I'll just go
home — but if my life is still
a movie, then I guess it's time
I stop watching it alone.

Boxed

Like dominos
I can see the boxes
That make up the sidewalks,
The many boxes
That drive on roads.
The boxes follow boxes,

Boxes swallow boxes,
Choices follow choices,
Consequently following
The same strain, like cars
Connecting into trains.

They collect and pile,
Then the towers topple,
Falling through the blocks
Going down
Down
The numbers
And rows,
As subsequent lists grow
More impatient,
Each crossed out day
Remaining perpetually listless.

I see the boxes
Inside boxes, living inside
Compartments,
The files, in folders,
On paper and screen.

Boxed,
Cataloged, yet lost,
Constantly watched
And never truly seen.

Hearts, Brains, and Guts

Don't listen to your heart;
It has a gambler's spirit.
Don't listen to your brain;
That holds too much merit.
But say you listen to your fear:
Both heart and brain close shut,
Then who else do you have to turn to
Except your nonexistent gut?
Do you listen to your heart?
Do you listen to your brain? Your gut?
These parts reign over the thoughts,
These hearts, brains, and guts.
Hearts, brains, and guts.

Face to Face

When I lifted
The mask from my face,
Nothing
Stared back at me. Expressionless and silent,
Nothing stared back at me. I touch,
But my fingers brush through the air.
I look down to my hands, and there,
On the bathroom counter,
My mask lays still. It glistens,
Seeming to listen, it holds
Tomorrow,
Molded to its shape,
It wears the undeniable mark
Of an uncertain fate.
I could've been someone else.
I laugh.
I could've been
Anyone else.
We stand face to face,
Once I've peeled it all away. And nothing
Stared back at me. Expressionless and indiscernible,
Nothing stared back at me.
I reach, but my fingers fall through the air,
Finding only nothing
Waiting for me there.

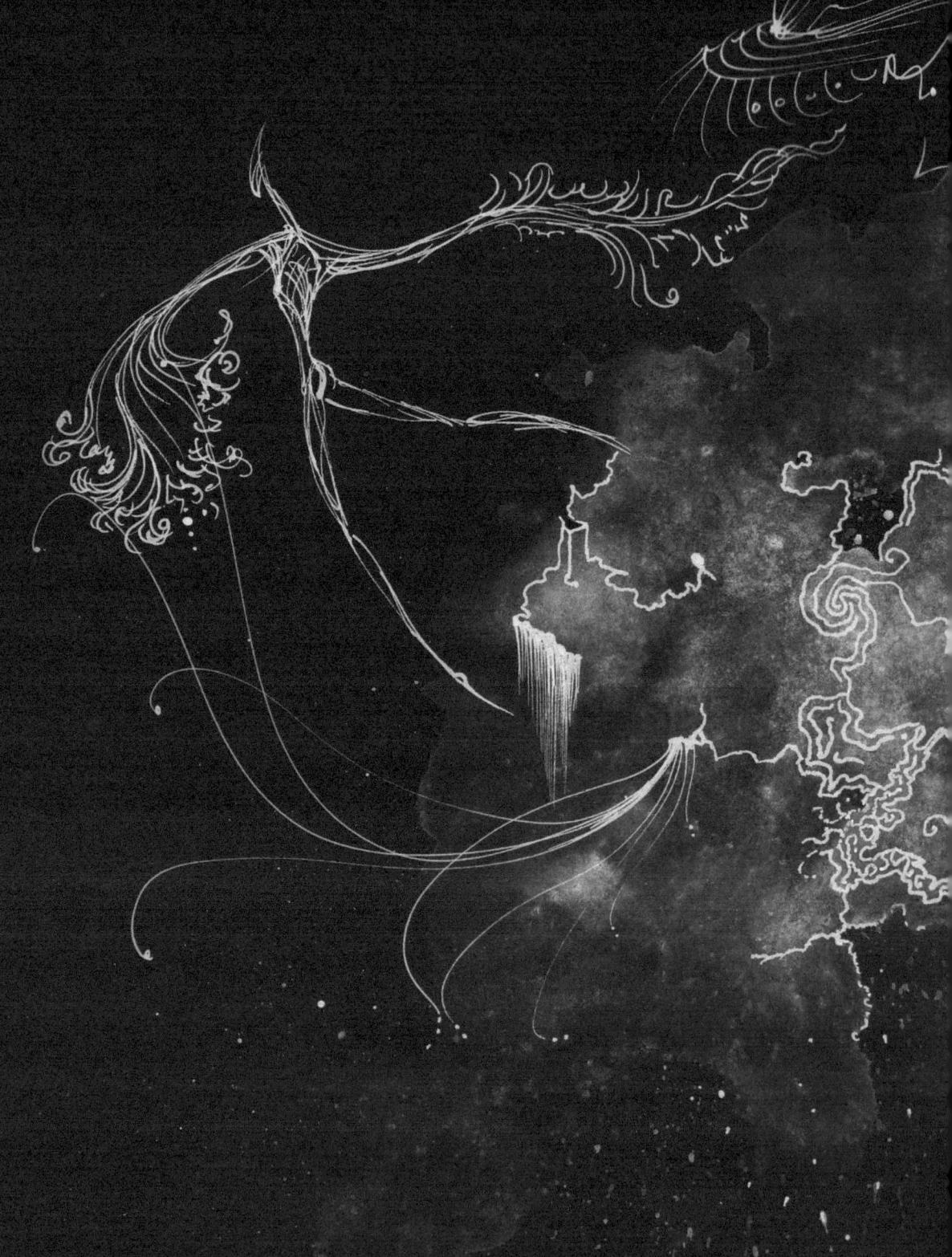

We Talk of Forever

I stay up all night and the ghosts
Of stars past
Still shine in the sky.
Forever is a feeling.
Forever is a lie—
It's the ultimate truth,
Nothing else is more true,
Not in the lowest Low
Or the happiest High.
And we talk of forever,
As if we really mean it,
We talk of forever
As if we'll ever see it.
But it's when I feel
Forever
That I finally believe it.
And so I stay up all night,
And then I live
Through my eyes.
Forever is a feeling,
Forever is when I fly.
When the ghosts
Of stars past
Still shine in the sky.

Time

It's never in my dreams
Nor lived out in thought.
It's never there where I am not.

I've tried,
But it can't be glimpsed, only felt,
And it can't be lived by
Someone else.

It's all that I've got,
Where I am somehow everything I am
And everything I'm not.
All these dreams
And all my thoughts.

73

Constellations

I still think about everyone I've ever met.
I wonder how they are,
I wonder who they really are —
Like so many memories,
I only take them out at night
When I can spread them out like stars,
So I can linger over each conversation,
Tracing pictures, faces,
Connecting constellations —

So I can think about
Everyone I've ever met,
As if I was ever important
To any of them.
So I can remember
All those who never really knew me
Whom I never really knew,
Wondering if anyone else is still thinking
Of me, too —

So I can look over
All these figures and constellations
Late into the evening,
So I can reread the stories,
Search for connection, for meaning,
Meeting everyone I've ever met,
All over
And over again.

Lovelorn

Late nights, early mornings
Spent alone with somber yearnings.
I want all and all of my pleas to come through.
But I wish all the lows wouldn't follow so soon.
I want all and all of my unease,
Give it all to me.
I want late nights and early mornings,
I want those wishful, lonely burnings.
Give them all to me,
To catch my dreams, then set them free.

Human

Is the door human?
Was its hinges' squeak
An attempt to speak?
Why is it not human anymore?

Is the streetlight human?
Is it looking down at me
From a glowing eye? Is it
A luminous fish in a watery sky?
Why is it not human anymore?

What about the bed?
What is that softness?
Is that it breathing
Underneath my head?
Is it dreaming alongside with me
As I lay tangled in its spread?

Is the night human?
Waiting to swallow me whole?
Is it empty and lonely like me?
Does it see me?
Does it have a soul?
Why is it not human anymore?

Chapter 4:

Spirit

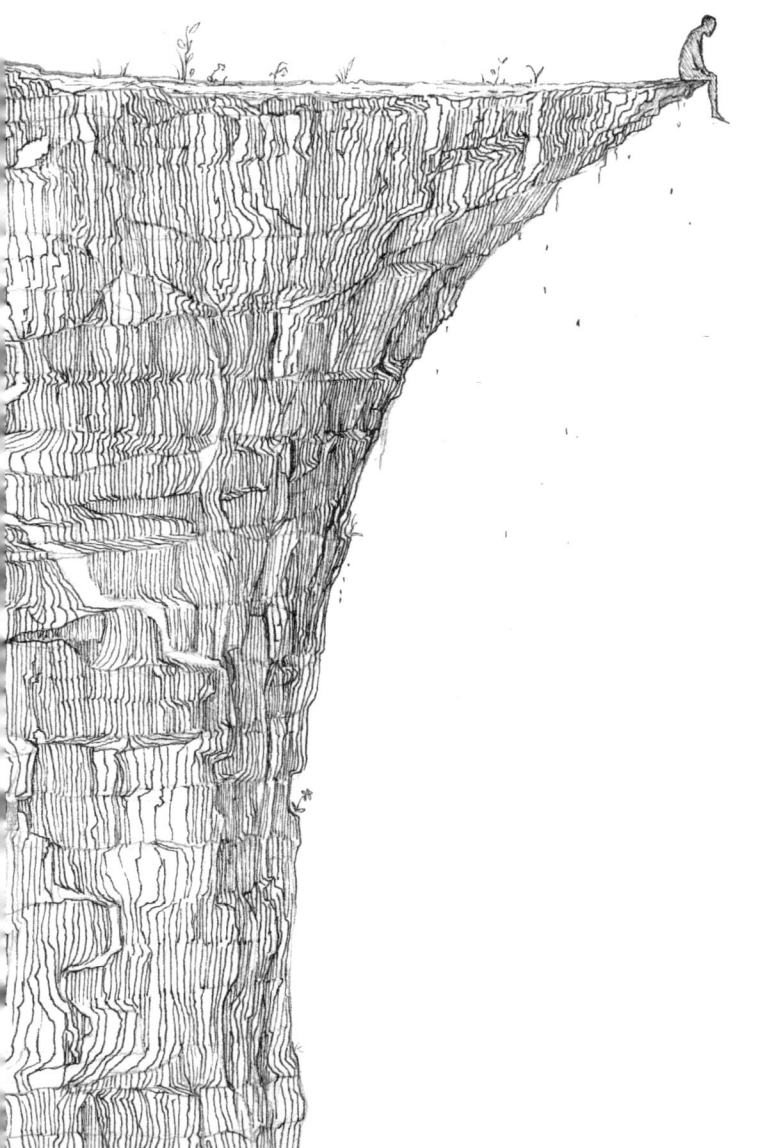

The Traveler

I've walked this earth
Looking for something
Wondrous and new,
But all I could find
Was the old
But true.

And the truth sits
At some precipice,
Precarious and carefree.
Everywhere I am,
Yet nowhere
I can be.

Like a Sunrise

She's a yawning, sleepy smile
Stretching farther every mile.
Lighting up the darkened floors
As she opens up pastel doors.

Like a Sunset

She's a wilting, shrinking flower
Shriveling smaller by the hour.
Instead of growing ever bolder,
At every glance she looks older.

Spring is First

Spring is first to take the leap,
Then Summer blooms, but
Is all too brief.
Autumn comes to turn a new leaf,
Then change, change and change
Is in the air.
Silence settles, as if it were always there,
And Winter arises,
Cold and fair.

Old Crow

I wonder what it's like
To be a crow
And to never know
What it's like to be a finch.
I wonder whether it's by nature or nurture
To speak by a caw
Or a cackle,
I wonder what it's like to be a murder,
But not a charm or a gaggle.
I wonder what it's like to be a crow
And to never know
If you are mistaken for the ravens,
The grackles, starlings,
Or the red-winged.
I wonder what it's like
To hear songs
You'll never sing.
Do you tune out the communal choir
That echoes in the leaves,
Preferring instead
To be the silhouette
At the top of the tree?
Do you fly high or lie low?
My little, wise friend,
Or the visage of death,
I wonder what it's like
To be a crow
And to never know
What it's like to be a finch.

Old Lore

Like two, tall redwoods
That had grown side by side.
Or like two, white wolves
Padding through
The snow
And the two sets of footsteps
They've left behind.

Two, long lines
Lighting the way up
The dark,
Empty street.
Maybe two falling leaves
That fell and never knew
They'd someday meet.

Yellow Butterflies

Before I was odd and peculiar,
Before I played the fool,
I was watching yellow butterflies
On the way to the pool.
With soapy hands waving wands,
Blowing bubbles into the blue,
Following the sun's light,
Watching clouds fade from view.
I want to go back to a time
When nothing mattered, when everything mattered.
I want to see the world again from a great height
And be trapped inside that bubble
Forever.
To be inside that little world
With me still
At its center.

The Phone Rings and Rings

The seat is left empty in the breeze
And it swings and swings
And swings...
But in my dreams, you still walk through the door.
In my dreams, everything
Is as it once was before.
Then in my dreams, we sway on swings,
And when the alarm goes off
The phone rings and rings and rings.

I hear the chimes
From somewhere deep
Where it will never reach.
Time passes slowly here
Like the moving shadow of a tree
As I close my eyes
And fall asleep...
And I sleep.

In my mind,
You still tell me your stories,
And in my eyes, you are still young.
In my dreams, you still walk through the door.
Then in my dreams, we sway on swings.
And when the alarm goes off,
The phone rings and rings and rings...

Those Who Have Not Forgotten

There are those who have not forgotten,
Who know that the work ahead is long,
So go to bed pained and bruised
To rise early in the dawn—

—To then go out into the wood,
Still sore and tired from the day before,
To come back to the same, un-felled tree,
To hack away at it once more.

Yet however burdened or downtrodden,
They always return to see it through—
But they who are happy are never those who still remember,
But those who've never forgotten why

They still do— they who wade through seas of changing leaves
To secure a world that they know cannot be kept—
The daily trek wearing a path like a bludgeon
To the heart of those who will never forget.

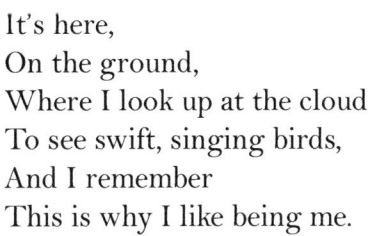

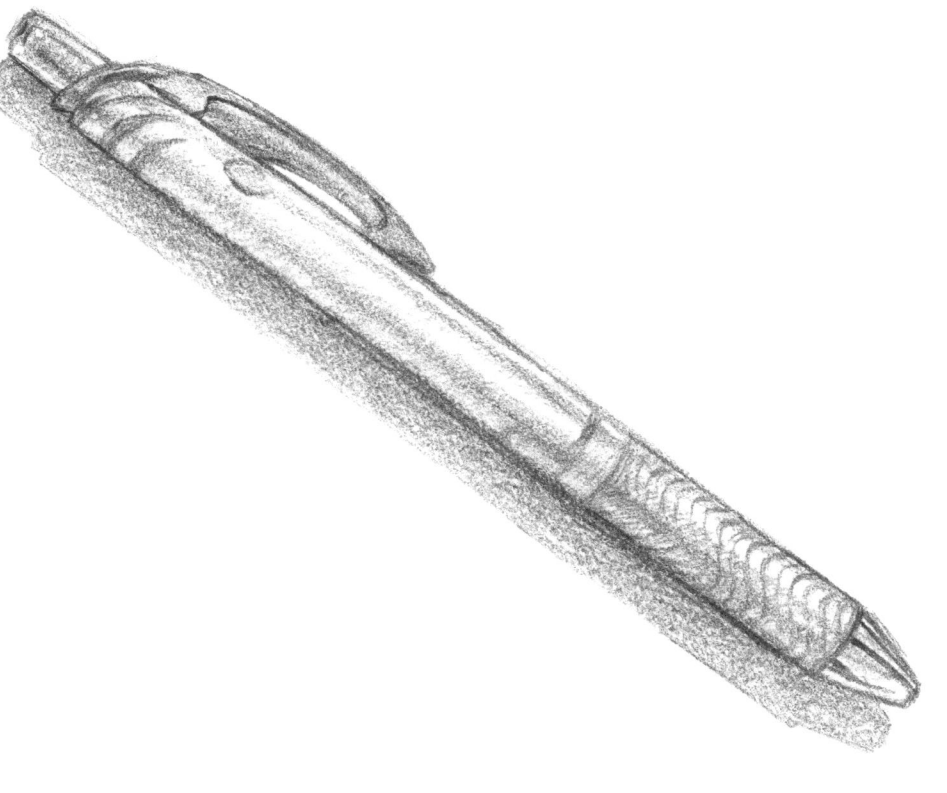

Falls Away

It's here,
On the ground,
Where I look up at the clouds
To see swift, singing birds,
And I remember
This is why I like being me.

Even with my spirit
That has sunk down to my feet.
I stand at the base of a great, green hill
And the air around me stands still,
I remember
Why I like being me.

When the world falls away,
When one can simply be
Is what I like most about being me.

The air soft and warm
When I'm walking all along the windy beach,
And I remember
Why I like being me.

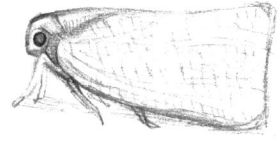

Ends

In one hand
There's always two.
In two hands
One's always cruel.

In one life
There's always two,
And neither lies
Nor tells the truth.

In one disguise
Are two lives,
In one soul,
There's always two.

In one end
There's always two.
One leading nowhere,
One somewhere new.

The Lone Wolf

Call me the lone wolf,
A far sea, a tide full,
A tall tree the wind pulls—
And I'll be the one proof,
That fate will be sure
To see through,
Of "never" meeting "forever"
The two you'd never seen together.
Forever and ever:
Never, never, never.

so Call me the lone wolf,
So the scrawl reads so in my book,
Sprawled weeds and dense woods,
A lost thief, the one aloof—
Call me the one pure—
That fate will be sure
To see through.
And like the better beneath this weather,
I will bow to it forever
And forever and ever—
Never, never, never!

I'm Fourteen and This is Deep

I wonder if our real lives
Are lived
Only in our sleep.
I'm fourteen and this is deep.

I still think so at sixteen,
But I'm nineteen,
And you can't keep living in your dreams.
We all have to grow up someday.
I'm twenty and this is deep.

It gets easier with time,
At twenty five,
Knowing to a greater extent
Than I've ever known before,
Only to realize that
I don't know anything
Once more—
At twenty nine, and this is deep.

I'm only getting old, I learn,
And not much wiser, and not any younger
At thirty three.
Yet it's only now that I know
That I was always
Younger than I believed.
I'm forty four and this is deep.

My forty eighth begins and
Though age settles in,
My health, family, and food
Keep me busy at fifty two.
It's funny, but
I feel as though
I'm constantly beginning anew
At fifty three, and this is deep.

And it still
Seems that way at fifty eight,
But I'm sixty three,
And life is short. There's no way back,
Only forward. Everyone dies.
Everyone grieves.
Nobody's invincible,
Or whatever else I used to think.
I'm sixty eight and this is deep.

Finding happiness in the present,
At seventy five,
I wonder if my life
Is lived most in sleep.
Perhaps fortune has been a lie.
Perhaps forgiveness is key.
I'm not sure.
Maybe I used to be.
I'm eighty one and this is deep.

In the End

Once you've been many people,
Once you've lived many lives
And lost them all,
Will all of it seem small?
When what once took forever,
When what once stood tall,
When what once took months and years
Will only take a few seconds to recall,
When what have once been seconds,
Become only one,
Will it all seem
As just a dream?
When what once was merely a dream,
Becomes a dream again
Once it's gone.

The Joke

"Life is a joke."
"Laugh, lest you cry,"
It's the kind of joke
That loses its fun
Once you ask too many
How's or why's.

"Life is just a joke,"
Find the humor in it, you say?
It's just a game we play
That plays us too,
"Humor life," my friend,
"And it may humor you."

Moments
Dancing
Slow

I have this moment.
So I fall in love with the moment.
I mean, sure, we go toe to toe,
But only 'cause we're dancing slow,
Knees weak, cheek to cheek,
The moment has them all beat.

So to and fro, we're dancing slow,
This moment melts away like snow.
Because this is fading, this is fleeting;
This is living, this is breathing.
This moment has them all beat,
This moment makes you weep,

And the moment feels eternal
Even as it passes
From moment to moment,
From sour to sweet.
I can't stop, can't speak,
This moment has them all beat.

Spirit

There is nothing else more fleeting
Than to feel a happy feeling.
Only true until it's gone,
Only the spirit can live on.

The Breath of the Beach

Animated by brush strokes,
The wind rolls across the sky.

With faint suggestions of lines,
A thicket of distant pines

Stand behind the greasy
And glistening
Surface of the water,
Smelling of oil paint.

I mix the colors
On my plate.

It lives...
In a wash of gray,
The humid, fishy
    Breath of the beach.

Coming up in sharp peaks,
    An imposing face

I touch

Of a cliff looks down
To the shaken
Spill of frothy waves
That lift up against the old stone
And glance off its weathered cheek.

100

Thick enough to coat
The back of a spoon,

While somewhere
In its depths

As if stirred,

Of clouds slowly swirl

Sails a pale, little ghost
Of a sickle shaped moon.

With a digit stained blue
High above
Where white daubs

101

That Poem

I am a Poem,
And I live within the paint of my words.
Rarely understood,
Forever searching for music that hasn't been heard.
Telling tales of things that only happen in dreams,
Attempting to recreate the way people think—
Aware that my words
Are permanent in the ink.
My time here is limited,
Yet somehow I must discover some truth.
Only to learn
That it's something that lies near the end,
Beyond my recalcitrant youth.
Only to eventually find
That there is no such thing as art
If it has not been overused.
But, I whittle away my time,
Hoping to leave some scuplture of a rhyme,
Because I am still a Poem,
And no matter how fleeting or bright,
It's all inescapably trite.
But even so,
I'll still be pining for that music
That forever plays inside.

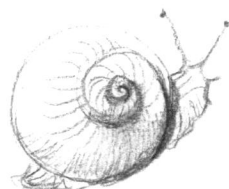

About the Author

E. Alen has been drawing and writing almost from
the first time she could pick up a pen. Since then,
she has been devoted to perfecting her art.
That Poem is her first book.

www.ingramcontent.com/pod-product-compliance
Lightning Source LLC
Chambersburg PA
CBHW040819120626

46551CB00005B/606